AUSTIN POWERS

How to Be an International Man of Mystery

by Michael McCullers

BANTAM BOOKS

LONDON · NEW YORK · TORONTO · SYDNEY · AUCKLAND

AUSTIN POWERS: HOW TO BE AN INTERNATIONAL MAN OF MYSTERY
A BANTAM BOOK: 0 553 50709 5

First publication in Great Britain

PRINTING HISTORY
Bantam edition published 1997

Austin Powers: International Man of Mystery screenplay by Mike Myers

Book design by Jackie Frant.

Bantam Books are published by Transworld Publishers Ltd,
61-63 Uxbridge Road, London W5 5SA,
in Australia by Transworld Publishers (Australia) Pty Ltd,
15-25 Helles Avenue, Moorebank, NSW 2170,
and in New Zealand by Transworld Publishers (NZ) Ltd,
3 William Pickering Drive, Albany, Auckland.

Reproduced, printed and bound in Great Britain by
Ebenezer Baylis & Son Ltd.

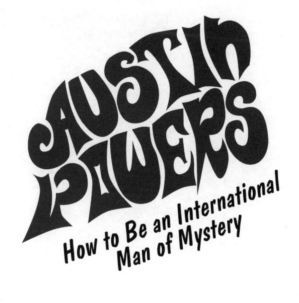

How to Be an International
Man of Mystery

Forward
by Austin Powers

Hello, hello.
Allow myself to introduce . . . myself.
My name is Austin Powers.
I'm a swinger by day,
and an International Man of Mystery by night.
Or sometimes just the opposite,
depending on if I get lucky.
(I don't even know what that means, baby!)
Although I don't work directly
for the British government, I am prepared
to volunteer service to Her Majesty
at the first sign of trouble.
Whether in the oil fields of the Middle East,
the frozen tundra of Russia,
or a dark men's room in a train station,

I never turn down a mission, and, just as importantly, I never miss the party afterwards, baby! Now, the editors of this manual have asked me to take a moment to be forward. I can't imagine why they'd want that in a serious tome like this one, but here goes:

"Hey, baby, would you like to go have a shag? You're a marvelous-looking bird, you are. We could have a long groovy shag in my jumbo jet. Whatever fits your schedule, baby! We could grab a quickie shag up against a wall like two crazed weasels, or we could shag in my Jag, or—"

Oh, sorry. Was I too forward? Excuse me one moment. (What? A different meaning of the word "forward"? You're yanking my cord, baby. Really? All right then.)

There we are. I'm back. I've just been informed by Basil Exposition, chief of British Intelligence, that what was needed was, in fact, a "foreword," a preface or introductory statement in a book, not "forward," meaning presumptuous, pert, or bold. An easy mistake, I'm sure you'll agree. After all, I have been frozen for thirty years, man.

Though my nemesis, Dr. Evil, is defeated for now, he is still at large. He will be back, baby, you can count on it. One day I myself might want to settle down, retire, get married (not bloody likely, man!), and then who will continue the fight against uptight squares? We need new swingers and International Men of Mystery. The price of swinging is constant vigilance, man. So, to all you swingers-in-the-making who want to be just like me, I say . . .

Behave!

Austin

2

A Word from Basil Exposition

My name is Basil Exposition, head of British Intelligence. You are reading a manual entitled, "How to Be an International Man of Mystery," by Austin Powers, presented by Boulevard Books. It is printed on fine-grade pulp paper using a version of Bodoni typeset developed at the University of Vienna. Perhaps I'm giving you too much information, but I like to be perfectly clear on what's happening at any given moment. A little over thirty years ago, I recruited a brash young swinger right off Carnaby Street. At the time, all he cared about was "wild shindigs" and "shagadelic birds," but I saw in him the makings of a fine operative. That swinger was Austin Powers. In the course of his career, Austin has served Her Royal Highness with distinction, and was granted the Order of the British Empire—the first swinger to be so honored. Perhaps you are wondering: if Austin was such an asset to the government, why did we accept his offer to be frozen for thirty years? That question can be answered in two words: Dr. Evil.

3

AUSTIN POWERS

Dr. Evil possesses the most fiendishly clever criminal mind ever to terrorize the earth. His ceaseless devotion to taking over the world is a threat to all the freedoms we hold dear. The only man who stopped Dr. Evil from achieving his nefarious goals was Austin Powers. After what appeared to be Austin's final defeat of Dr. Evil in 1967, the mad genius escaped into orbit around the Earth. No one doubted he would return; it was only a matter of when.

Austin bravely volunteered to have himself frozen in anticipation of that dark day. Leaving family and friends behind, Austin entered cryogenic storage thirty years ago. None of us had any idea it would take three decades, but Dr. Evil has indeed returned.

Thus, we have unfrozen our own secret weapon. Austin is experiencing many side effects from the unfreezing, including dry mouth, fever, disorientation, and flatulence at moments of extreme relaxation, but we fully expect him to complete his mission successfully and rid the world of Dr. Evil. Then we expect him to get some dental work—caps, braces, bleaching, the whole show.

Without further ado, here he is—Austin Powers, International Man of Mystery.

—Basil Exposition
British Intelligence

INTERNATIONAL MAN OF MYSTERY THEME

There are very few hard-and-fast rules concerning international espionage, but here's one of them: every spy worth his salt has a catchy theme song. There's nothing quite like it for setting the mood— for danger, or for love. Behave!

Here's my theme. I wrote it with my friend Burt Bacharach on a schooner near Majorca just after Yom Kippur. You know, the usual. Enjoy!

International Man of Mystery
He's the most swingiest cat in history.
He can't be limited to one country,
And people don't know a lot about him.
He has testicles and a penis,
Therefore, he's called—
International Man of Mystery!
The exact opposite of him would be
Regional woman of familiarity.
But, of course, that's not to be,
Because he's the—
International Man of Mystery!
He's the International Man—
He's the International Man—
He's the International Maaaaaaaaan ...
of Mystery!

Austin Powers's Secrets of Disguise

"Special Bonus Insert:
Austin Powers's
Secrets of Disguise!"

An International Man of Mystery
never goes anywhere without his disguise kit.
At any time, the Queen could call me away to
some exotic location, and my motto is
"Be prepared, baby!"
You'd be surprised at the transformation
which can occur with a few well-chosen articles
of clothing and the proper technique.

Observe:

Sometimes all it takes
is a few accessories to
complete a disguise.
No one would
recognize me as a
ghastly American tourist.

6

7

Shag is a many-splendored word. Many times, when I'm at a loss on how to express a difficult sentiment, I just slip in the word shag and it all falls into place. Noun, verb, adjective—it doesn't matter, baby! Because when you're talking in Shag, you're speaking the language of love.

If you're at a party, and it's particularly groovy, I mean, it's really happening, you might say it's shagadelic, or perhaps, shagerrific.

If you're with your bird at a club and she starts laughing, and that gets you to laughing which sets off another cat laughing, then you'd say, "Baby, your laughter is shagtagious."

If you can't get enough—I mean like a nymphomaniac or a Swedish girl—then you're shag-mad, baby! Join the club! If you find that you can't stop shagging, however, and that people are beginning to talk about your shagging at work, then you might have a problem. You might be shagaddicted. Recognizing your problem is the first step to recovery, my friend. Good luck.

A quick shag is a sha—

A vertical shag might be up against a wall, for instance.

A shag in your Jag would be a shag-on-wheels.

A shag on your jumbo jet is a mile-high shag.

8

If I formed a nation, I would call it Shagtavia. The form of government would be a shagocracy, ruled by the person with the most shagocity. The shaganomic system would be Marxist, with each person giving according to ability and receiving according to need, if you know what I mean, baby!

Shag can even be used in anger, as in, "shag off!" or "Leave me the shag alone!"

If things aren't quite right, you might say they're shaggedly-waggedly. If you overdo it a bit, you might call yourself shagged out (though I don't speak from experience here, baby!).

I've heard that you Yanks do something called "shagging flies." I don't even want to know what that it is, man. You Americans are kinky buggers!

Well, until we shag again—
Shagfully yours,

Austin

Mrs. Kensington, mother of the ever-lovely Vanessa, was my loyal partner back in the sixties. Together we battled the forces of evil all over the globe and attended many a swinging shindig. Mrs. K had a mind like a steel trap, a vicious roundhouse kick, and she filled out her leather fightsuit very nicely indeed.

Orwellian, ironic statement on the spectre of man-made electronic media techno-fascism gone awry. It makes you look like a clapped-out whore, who, in her late twenties, is trying to hold on to the flower of her youth, and in doing so ironically becomes the faded ingenue she most feared turning into."

A WORD ABOUT MRS. K

In all the years we worked together, we only had one fight, and it was quite a drag, man. What happened was, Mrs. K came over to my loft sporting a ghastly new haircut from the trendiest salon on Carnaby Street.

She asked me what I thought of it, and I said, "I think it's unflattering, baby."

She said, "Thank you for your honesty, Austin. It's refreshing."

So I said, "In that case, it's over-styled and unnecessarily rococo—a poor man's version of Sassoon, in the sense that it mimics the current trend of rejecting the so-called natural look in favor of an almost Brechtian, alienating,

It turns out that perhaps I was a bit *too* honest, baby. Mrs. K gave me one of her patented roundhouse kicks right into the pubis. Gor blimey, boys, I didn't walk for three days!

All in all, however, we got along like a dog and his bone. (Behave!) People always want to know if we shagged. She was married and she was my partner, man. It wouldn't have been right. Plus, she never let me!

So here's to you, Mrs. K! You're still "It," baby!

Here's where I destroyed Dr. Evil's underwater lair and foiled his plans to poison the world's oceans with deadly asbestos.

Here's where I destroyed Dr. Evil's ice lair and foiled his plans to contaminate the world's fuel supply with deadly Spam. (Yes, Spam in our fuel. Think of the chaos.)

This is Hawaii. My dad would never set foot on Hawaii because they murdered Captain Cook. "Poor Captain Cook," he'd say, "the bloody Hawaiians, they murdered him in his bloody sleep." My dad wouldn't even have a pineapple in the house, on account of what the Hawaiians did to Captain Cook. My dad was a difficult man to understand.

Here's where I destroyed Dr. Evil's mountain lair and foiled his plans to pollute the world's rain forests with deadly household cleanser.

Here's where I destroyed Dr. Evil's underground lair and foiled his plans to set off the world's volcanoes with a nuclear probe. More importantly, here's where I got to know Vanessa. And I got to know her very well, indeed. Behave!

Here's a map of the world, showing all the countries I've visited in my travels. As you can see, between my missions for the Queen and my general jet-setting swinger lifestyle, I've been to every single country on the globe, man.* Isn't that smashing?

Around the World

*Except Canada. Inexplicably, I've never been there. Burundi, French Guinea, even Sri Lanka (formerly Ceylon), but never Canada. Apparently there just isn't much call for an International Man of Mystery there—no madmen on the loose, very few evil corporations, not even much towel-stealing from hotel rooms. I hear Toronto is a paradise, however, and the literacy rate is the highest in the world.

11

TOP Ten Birds, THEN and NOW

A lot of things have changed since the sixties (Does anybody remember Ovaltine? It seemed like a good idea at the time), but there's still a lot of great-looking birds around. It's a good thing, too, or I wouldn't know what to do with myself. I might have to develop other interests, even get a hobby or something—the thought of it is simply ghastly.

Obviously the nineties chicks are still new to me,
but I've been watching the telly and going to the cinema,
so I'll do my best (and my best ain't bad, baby!).
Here's my notion of the most shagadelic birds, then and now:

Then:

Twiggy — (What can I say, man? Thin was in.)

Jane Fonda — (Jane's a square? I guess things *have* changed.)

Emma Peel — (She's got a lot of appeal. In fact, I'd like to a-peel her a-clothes off, baby!)

Raquel Welch — (Nobody looks better in animal skin than the Rock, man!)

Brigitte Bardot — (Bardot oh, oh, oh!)

Jacqueline Bisset — (Do yourself a favor, lad, don't miss it!)

Sophia Loren — (I've always had a weakness for Italian delicacies.)

Ursula Andress — (If she doesn't make you horny, then you don't have blood in your body!)

Jackie O — (Aristotle and I almost came to blows over her, man.)

The Queen — (It's my duty.)

NOW:

Björk — (The birds are hot in Iceland.)

Elizabeth Hurley — (She's English *and* she has perfect teeth!)

Hillary Clinton — (Power is an aphrodisiac, baby!)

RuPaul — (An African goddess, man! Strong, yet ladylike.)

Baywatch girls — (I can't tell them apart, but gor blimey! I almost ruptured my spleen when they came on the telly!)

Demi Moore — (She frightens me, but she makes me very randy, indeed!)

JFK Jr.'s wife — (Like father, like son. Well done, John-John!)

Jacqueline Bisset — (She's like that bunny on the telly— she just keeps going and going.)

Elisabeth Shue — (I'd like to be her Karate Kid! Behave!)

13

Austin's Jaguar XKE

Here she is, the woman in my life—my 1967 convertible Shaguar. She's outfitted with the usual amenities: Connolly leather hides, disc brakes all around, a powerful 4.2-litre engine, but, as you can see, I had the boys at Coventry install a few "special options."

The steering wheel is on the *right*, of course, because here in England (and in Japan and Australia) we drive on the *right* side of the road, which is the left. That is not to say that Americans, who drive on the *right* side of the road, drive on the *wrong* side of the road, but rather that we English drive on the other side of the road, neither *wrong* nor *right*, but *left*. Although I for one believe it is the *right* side of the road, which neither states nor implies that the *right* side is the *wrong* side, or the *left* side is the correct side, but merely suggests that the *right* side is not, actually, the *right* side. Damn, I've gone cross-eyed.

Just look at the lines of my Jaguar, the way the rear haunches are poised for action, the long feminine curves of the bonnet, leading to the seductive scoop of the grille, nesting the headlights like firm, round . . .

Does that make you horny? Does it? Does that car make you horny? The shape of it? It makes me randy indeed!

In the course of my thirty-year career as an
International Man of Mystery, I've hobnobbed with
some of the world's richest and most powerful people.
I won't lie to you, man, it's been a gas!
But sometimes you're at a reception, meeting yet another
head of state, or having a schnapps with the Queen,
and you feel lonely all of a sudden and you just want to
hang out with your mates, you know, just be normal.
In times like that I go over to Mick Jagger's house and
party with the Stones. Always keep in touch with the
common man, baby.

16

Austin with Celebs

17

I love naughty engravings, baby!
They make me laugh, and
they also make me horny.
You can't ask for much more
than that out of life, man.
If one of them strikes your fancy,
you might want to give it
to someone you love.
Get it? "Give it"
to someone you love?
A bit of the old in-and-out?
Behave!

Naughty Engravings

"A BIT OF ALL RIGHT!"

19

CHEESES OF THE WORLD

Collector's Plate

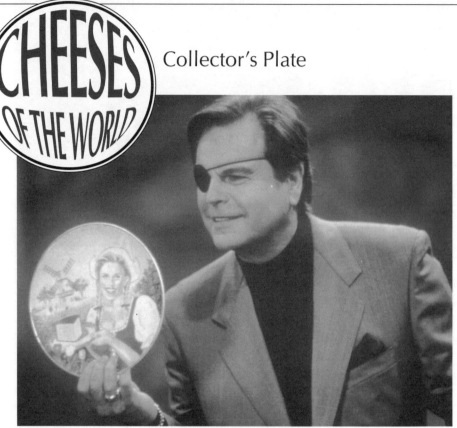

Now is your chance to own a piece of history.
Our hand-painted theme plates are perfect for decorating,
gift-giving, or collecting.

Production will be limited to just forty-five firing days, so act fast.
Send your first monthly payment of $29.95 and we'll ship you your
theme plate, with a full money-back guarantee.

A special note to collectors: some plates, like the Cheeses of the World
series, have gone up in value as much as 240 percent.*

The Franklin Mint
a Virtucon corporation

*As with any investment, there is some risk involved.

A word about
CHOPPERS

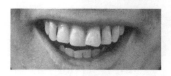

Since I've been unfrozen, I've heard a lot about the state of my choppers. Gor blimey! You'd think from all this talk that they're the worst you've ever seen. Well, let me explain something. In Britain, in the sixties, you could have bad teeth and still be a sex symbol. It didn't matter, man. We were free and without judgment. We weren't so hung up on this "dental hygiene" thing, baby. But, in the interest of fitting in, I went to Basil Exposition's dentist for a checkup.

Here's what Dr. Saul Pressner had to say:

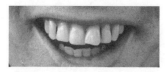

"What we have here is the classic result of a lifetime of neglect in the area of dental

hygiene and preventative care. In medical terms . . . well, it's bad, very bad. The recommended course of therapy would include caps, bonding, filling, bleaching, root canals, bridges, and breaking the jaw in order to reset it at the proper alignment."

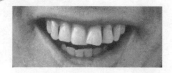

Bloody unlikely, I said. Instead, I've set about to change people's prejudices based on dental condition. Remember, hate comes from fear, and people fear what they don't know. In the interest of furthering human brotherhood and ridding the world of tooth bias, I ask, don't hate us because we're different. Your best friend might have bad teeth.

How to Dance

Sometimes, squares like to pretend like they're swingers. You see it all the time at the clubs—some old geezer looking at the young birds and thinking, "this free love is a bit of all right!" A banker might have the right clothes, the right car, even the right haircut, but he's still a square at heart, baby!

The easiest way to tell a square in swinger's clothing is the way he dances. Squares just sway right and left and they never move their feet. To be a swinger, you have to groove!

Dancing is all about freedom, man. You've got to free your mind and follow the musical vibes to a groovy plane of existence. Do you follow so far? Here are a few pointers on how to dance like a swinger. Feel free to improvise, but BE CAREFUL! Some of my more powerful moves have been known to cause chicks' heads to explode.

It doesn't matter what you look like as long as you've got a groovy lingo. Here are a few of my faves:

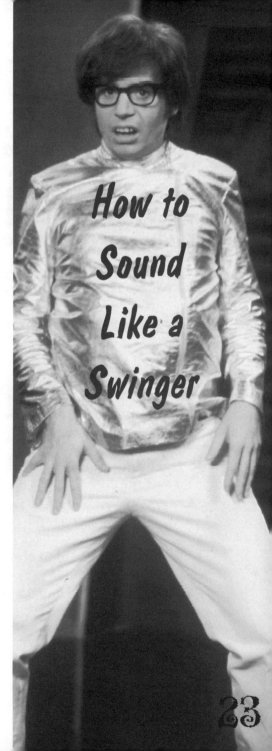

How to Sound Like a Swinger

behave!	admonition to cease sexual innuendo
shag	n,v,adj, adv, sexual intercourse; see also: shag some crumpet
randy	horny, excited, blood-engorged
what a gas!	what a swell time!
dosh	money, cash; also: cabbage, green
gor blimey!	an expression of extreme emotion; the closest translation might be "oh, my!"; from the ancient English "Gods blind me!"
choppers	teeth
jobblies	bosom, breasts, esp. large ones; see: randy
cat	chap, fellow, man, esp. a popular one
saucy	cheeky
cheeky	saucy
fab	great, in style
gear	in fashion, popular
thrombo	heart attack; usually used in the negative: "Don't have a thrombo, man!"
strumpet	slut, whore
odds and sods	errands
switched on	in the know, part of the in scene
square	see: Dr. Evil
hang-ups	things that make you uptight about shagging
turn-ons	things that make you want to shag (like go-go boots or school-girl outfits or, given the right mood, a crack in the pavement)
village bike	a loose girl, a harlot (as in "she's the village bike—everyone's had a ride")
rancid	unshaggable (extremely rare)
cracking Judy	a good-looking bird

HOW GOOD A SHAG ARE YOU?

1. How large is your jumbo jet?

A) Average   (5 points)
B) Much larger than average   (You're lying, but good on ya! 10 points)
C) Average length, but very wide   (0 points)

2. How many times a week, on average, do you shag?

A) 10   (3 points)
B) 30   (7 points)
C) Wilt Chamberlain   (Hello, hello! 10 points)

3. How many people, on average, are in the room when you shag?

A) 1   (0 points; see question 9)
B) 2   (3 points)
C) Including stewardesses?   (10 points, baby!)

4. Are you a member of the mile-high club?

A) Yes   (10 points)
B) No   (0 points)
C) What's the mile-high club?   (-5 points)

5. How many times a day do you think about shagging?

A) 1–15   (2 points)
B) 16–30   (5 points)
C) What? What were you saying?   (10 points)

6. Does this questionnaire make you horny?

A) No   (Is there no blood in your body? 0 points)
B) Somewhat   (5 points)
C) Very randy indeed!   (I'm like a rutting dear myself! 10 points)

7. Are you Italian?

A) Si   (5-point bonus)
B) No   (Sorry. 0 points)

8. Have you shagged chicks from exotic locations where the postage stamps are irregularly shaped?

A) Yes   (Well done. 5 points)
B) No   (Work on it. 0 points)
C) Does Cleveland count?   (Absolutely! 10 points)

9. Do you masturbate?

A) Yes   (Thank you for being honest. 5 points)
B) No   (Bloody liar. 5 points)

TOTAL: _____

Add up your total points. If you have—

0–60 points, turn to page 82
65–75 points, turn to page 27
More than 80 points, turn to page 101

25

More About Sea Bass

Only recently, I narrowly escaped becoming the dinner of Dr. Evil's vicious underwater friends. No, not piranha. Not sharks either, or barracuda. What we faced was much worse. Sea bass, baby! Mutated and ill-tempered. I took some time to find out more about sea bass, and it might surprise you to learn that they're among the ocean's most lethal killers. And I mean without any mutations or altered moods, baby. To find out more about these deadly bass, I went to *The Encyclopedia Piscalogica,* edited and translated from the original Bavarian by my good friend Marco Schnabel, a world-renowned expert on all things fishy and not a half-bad jazz pianist once you get a few Schnapps into him. Here's what I learned:

Sea Basses (or is it just Sea Bass in the plural? Or perhaps Sea Bassae? Or maybe Sea Bice? Good lord, now I've got a headache!) are more formally known by their scientific name, *Serranidae.* Of course, it's hard to know a sea bass formally—they're very casual, running around in their knickers and that sort of thing. Anyway, back to my point. Sea bass are found most often in oceans and seas, and hardly ever in fresh water. I myself prefer fresh water, as the salt water often makes me regurgitate after I swallow several gallons of it. And, of course, the salt burns terribly as it shoots out of my nose. I should have mentioned that I'm not a very good swimmer. Anyway, the sea bass is a large fish, with a wide body and bands of very sharp teeth. Their heads are often covered with scales (I myself had this problem until I found a special shampoo at the chemist's). Somehow this has all been about me, and not sea bass. I can't help it, baby, I fascinate myself.

Remember, if you come face to face with a sea bass, just don't *lose your head.* You've got to stay a *head* of them! That's the only way to get a *head* in life! Otherwise, you'll never be the *head* of a major corporation! Sorry.

"HELLO HELLO!"

27

Mad Libs

Dr. Evil's Mad Lib:

Hello, gentlemen. I've gathered you here in my (adjective) lair in (location) to tell you about my newest plan to take over the (noun). I plan to use highly (adjective) materials stolen from Fort (noun) in the heart of (location) to (verb) the world's (noun) supply. (Number) people will die unless the United (plural noun) pays me (number) dollars within (number) hours. The only man who can (verb) me is Austin Powers, and I've set a trap for that (adjective) swinger in the (body part) Club in (location). As soon as I have him in my (plural body part) I'll put him in the deadly (noun) trap, where he'll be suspended over a (container) of (plural animal) until he (bodily function) his pants.

Austin's Mad Lib:

As I was (-ing verb) on Carnaby Street last (day of the week) I saw a groovy Nehru (article of clothing) that would match my (noun) quite well. I (verb) into the shop, called the Happening (type of fruit), and looked at all the (adjective) items, which were priced quite (adverb). But what really caught my (body part) was the (adjective) bird working behind the counter. She had large blue (body parts) and (adjective) hair. I thought, "now there's the type of chick who likes to (verb) and likes to do it (number) times a day!" As I was standing there thinking whether to shag or (verb), she turned and said, "Hi there, (type of serviceman), you've got a beautiful (body part)." It was then I realized that this bird was actually a (animal)! I should have known, because you can always tell by the large (body part). That'll teach you not to judge a (noun) by its cover, baby!

29

JET-SETTERS

The Magazine for Today's Happening Groovy Flyers

Look inside for:
Today's best buy for
a corporate plane

SPECIAL BONUS:
An interview with Austin Powers
and a look at his stewardesses
from around the world

30

"If You See This Jet

A' Rockin' Don't Come A' Knockin'!"

While owning your own private jet is not a prerequisite for being an International Man of Mystery, it is *extremely* groovy. With my own jet I can be in Buenos Aires fighting crime during the day and still make it to a happening shindig in Chelsea that night. My favorite part of having a private jet is the bevy of sexy stews that comes with it.

I go mad for sexy stews, especially those groovy fly girls who ask, "Coffee, tea or me?" I can only respond: "Yeah, baby, yeah!" And when one says, "Fly me!" it makes me very randy indeed!

continued next page

*H*ow would they fit into
the shagadelic uniforms
I had designed especially for
me by my friend Halston?

*A*pparently in the nineties,
not all stewardesses are chicks,
and they're not even called
stewardesses anymore—
they're "flight attendants" now.
To each his own, man, but
blokes on a jumbo jet don't
do a damn thing for me.

Everyone knows that going through customs is the biggest drag about flying. Here's a news flash—you've got to do it even if you have your own private jet. I was surprised when I first heard it too. Anyway, they're always asking the same square questions. Here's how I handle it:

Customs Official:
"Step up, please."

Me:
"Hello, hello."

Customs Official:
"Traveling from what country?"

Me:
"Jolly old England!"

Customs Official:
"So your name is Danger Powers?"

Me:
"No, my name is Austin Powers. Danger is my middle name."

Customs Official:
"Are you carrying any illegal contraband?"

Me:
"Baby, I *am* the illegal contraband!"

Customs Official:
"What's your occupation?"

Me:
"I'm an International Man of Mystery."

Customs Official:
"What exactly does an International Man of Mystery do?"

Me:
"If I told you, I'd no longer be an International Man of Mystery, would I?"

At about this point, they usually take me into a small gray room with no windows and do a painful search of my rectal vault. On second thought, I'd recommend just filling out the form quickly and quietly, with a minimum of sarcasm.

HOW TO BUY A PRIVATE JET

Here are a few pointers for you International Men of Mystery with the resources to buy your own private jet. For those of you who don't have the dosh, start saving now. It's worth it, man! You haven't lived until you join the mile-high club!

Austin's Private Jet

Manufacturer: .... Boeing
Type: .... 747 wide-body
Year Manufactured: 1967
Length: .... 284'8"
Wingspan: .... 190'
Top Speed: .... 412 mph
Crew: .... 4 sexy stews (or 3 if they're Swedish—I'm only one man, baby!)
Special Features: .... Dual 8-track stereo decks (in quad— groovy!); built-in movie projectors, 35mm and Super 8 (for the "art" films, of course); fully stocked wet bar (flying makes me a bit nervous, so I usually have a couple of stiff Skinny Pirates en route); fully adjustable beanbag chairs; revolving circular bed; psychedelic paint job with Austin Powers logo

1. Make sure it's a jumbo, baby, or else there's no point! You've got to have room to party.

2. Used jumbo jets are acceptable, particularly when the previous owners were royalty. I find that Arab potentates offer the best prices.

3. Look for a jet with shag carpeting already in place. You'll save a bundle!

4. Make sure that the engine mount flange bolts have been renewed, in accordance with OSHA Safety Bulletin #474A. If not, the engine could shear off and you'll die in a giant fireball, baby! That's not too groovy!

5. Wait a day before you make your decision. There's nothing worse than buying a jumbo jet on impulse and regretting it the morning after.

THINGS TO LOOK FOR WHEN SHOPPING FOR A JET

Good flying, baby!

35

MATCHING GAME

Here's a sophisticated psychological test that I developed to help Basil and the boys at British Intelligence find the top-notch applicants to the International Man of Mystery program. Match the phrase on the left with its meaning from the list on the right. Be careful—it's more tricky than it looks. Good luck, baby!

1. Wedding Tackle	A. Penis
2. Twig and Berry	B. Penis
3. Little Elvis	C. Penis
4. Jobblies	D. Penis
5. Bits and Pieces	E. Penis
6. Tool Kit	F. Breasts
7. Meat and Two Veg	G. Penis
8. Tallywhacker	H. Penis

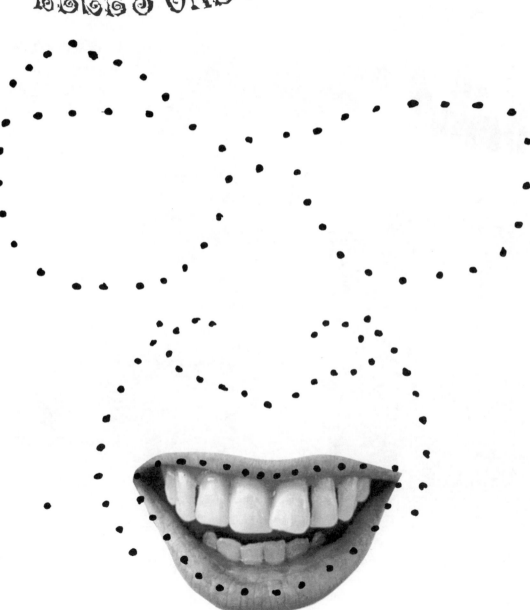

37

Does That Make You Horny?

A number of common items make me randy indeed!
Just the shape of them makes me horny.
To me, they are Eros manifest.
How about you?

Look at that! Does that make you horny? It's Big Ben! Do you have blood in your body? Just the name alone makes me randy.

Hello, hello! It's a selection of delightfully evocative natural formations. Enough said.

Look at the arm,
so long and erect.
And that torch, baby, it's
not the only thing on fire!
Good on ya, Yanks!

Neither of these items
separately makes me
horny in the least.
Put them together,
however, and I
become downright
blood-engorged!

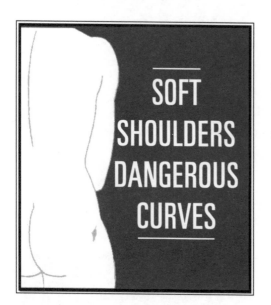

SOFT
SHOULDERS
DANGEROUS
CURVES

Soft shoulders and dangerous curves?
That reminds me of Brigitte Bardot
and if that doesn't make you horny, you
must not have a heart beating in your body!

Now see, this doesn't do a bloody
thing for me. It doesn't make me
horny at all. Must be some sort
of misfire in the libido, I dunno.

Now, after all this wild
excitement, you better
turn to page 15.

HANG-UPS & TURN-ONS

The goal of every good swinger is to eliminate hang-ups and find new turn-ons. My guru once told me every turn-on is also a turn-in. You tell me what that means, baby, because I haven't got a clue!

Only a square lets his hang-ups get in the way of a good shag, but even an accomplished swinger like myself has a few peccadilloes. (Does that word make you horny? Does it? Say it out loud, it sounds dirty! Just look at it, the shape of it. It makes me randy, indeed!)

Here's a list of my hang-ups and turn-ons:

Turn-ons:
- walking on the beach in Brighton
- the sound of rain against the windows
- Ravel's *Bolero*
- hospitals (there's nurses in there, you know)
- subtitled movies (more often than not, there's Swedish girls in them, baby)
- liberated chicks
- large jobblies (I'm only human, baby!)
- trains entering tunnels
- the smell of plastic
- nuns' habits (what? is that so wrong?)

Hang-ups:
- moles with hairs in them
- man's inhumanity to man

Let's see, that's about all the hang-ups I can think of right now.
Like I said, baby, don't let the mind games get in the way of a good shag!

What I like best about the nineties:

racial harmony

pay-at-the-pump gasoline

all these new channels on the telly

political rhetoric without
    cold war posturing

the Wonderbra

dirty pictures on this thing called
    the Internet

beer balls

the scanner guns at the supermarket

Hooters

RuPaul (she's shagadelic, baby!)

What I like least about the nineties:

cellular phones

war ain't over, baby

no jet packs or flying cars

health clubs

all these new channels on the telly

even more squares than in the fifties

finding out about RuPaul

all this hullabaloo about dental hygiene

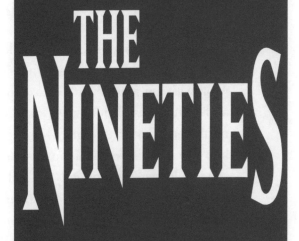

THE NINETIES

Before I met Agent Vanessa Kensington,
I thought I would never settle down. It
was against my swinger's credo, baby.
I thought the ocean was full of birds,
you know what I mean? Don't worry,
I haven't gone square. I still swing, it's
just that these days I swing with one
chick instead of twenty.

A Word About Vanessa

I have to admit, it wasn't quite love
at first sight. When I first saw Vanessa,
what with her glasses and release forms
and regulations, I thought, "Gor blimey,
nerd alert!" Later, though, when I got to
know her, I realized what an absolutely
shagadelic person she really was. She's
Oxford-educated, fluent in fourteen
languages, proficient in the use of most
firearms, and she's got legs that go all
the way down to the floor, if you know
what I mean.

I have known many birds, but
none more groovy than Vanessa. She's
turned this swinger into a one-woman
International Man of Mystery.

Back in the sixties, my assistant Reg kept my schedule. It was no easy task, I assure you—I was a cat on the go! go! go!

I gave Reg a tinkle on the telling bone when I was unfrozen, but it turns out that he now owns a special-interest bookshop called Mates with his friend Daniel. I asked Reg if he had a wife and kids and he said, "Austin, I'm gay." "Reg," I said, "Being happy is important, but family is everything as you get older."

The long and short of it is that Reg is no longer available, so I've got to keep my own schedule. No problem, baby! Vanessa's given me something called a Filofax that should fit the bill nicely. Good on ya!

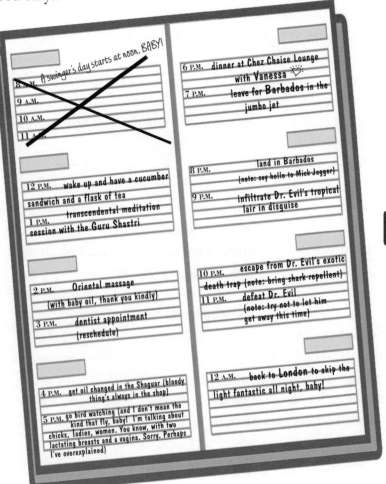

A Day
in the
Life
of an
International
Man
of
Mystery

51

Know Your Enemy

Being an International Man of Mystery isn't all fun and games, baby. Sure, jet-setting off to exotic locales is exciting, as is driving the finest automobiles, eating at the swankiest restaurants, and hobnobbing with royalty. And yes, shagging the world's most beautiful birds is quite groovy as well. But, all that aside, being an International Man of Mystery is really about fighting evil. That's our mission, our brief, our raison d'être, baby!

There's no more villainous cat around than our Dr. Evil. I had myself frozen thirty years ago because I knew he'd be back. Sure enough, he reentered Earth's atmosphere and now he's threatening the nineties. The bad Doctor is motivated by one thing, man—greed. He's the ultimate square, baby, and he must be stopped!

We don't know a whole lot about Dr. Evil, just that his fiendishly genius mind never stops scheming about ways to take over the world, often using bizarre doomsday devices. Through crack research by British Intelligence, and the brave sacrifice of more than one good agent, we've managed to collect the following information on Dr. Evil.

Be careful, baby—we consider him armed and *very* square!

Transcription of Dr. Evil's Therapy

One of our most valuable tools for getting inside Dr. Evil's head (and what a square head it is, baby!) has been a top-secret recording of a group therapy session involving him and his son, Scott. One of the other group members was actually an agent for British Intelligence. Unfortunately, Dr. Evil caught on to our little gambit, and had the group liquidated. Here is a transcription of that recording. Take a journey into the mouth of evil, if you dare.

DR. EVIL
...my childhood was typical. Summers in Rangoon, luge lessons.
In the spring we'd make meat helmets. If I was insolent, I was
placed in a burlap bag and beaten with reeds. Pretty standard,
really. At the age of twelve I received my first scribe. At the
age of fifteen, a Zoroastrian named Vilma ritualistically
shaved my testicles. There really is nothing like a shorn
scrotum. At the age of eighteen, I went off to evil medical
school. From there—

SCOTT EVIL
(interrupting)
See! See how he is? He's a nutbar!

THERAPIST
Scott, try to make your point without name-calling.

SCOTT
All this stuff he talks about is crazy, you know? It's like
this all the time—blah, blah, blah! He's always talking about
taking over the world and whatever. I just want to be normal,
you know?

THERAPIST
Dr. Evil, Scott has expressed a wish to fit in, to be like
other people his age, which is absolutely appropriate for
someone at his stage of development. Is this something you
can provide him?

DR. EVIL
Well, it's true—my tastes are rather exotic. Have you ever
heard of the enguava fruit? It cures the common cold. It's very
rare. I have three. The Balinese government has the only
other one. When I was growing up we kept monkeys as pets; also

lemurs, sloths, tapirs, what have you. I enjoy rarities.
May I offer you a cigar? Pre-Castro Davidoff. I own one hundred
and thirty-eight of them. Arnold and Letterman own the others.
For now.

THERAPIST
There's no smoking in this building, Dr. Evil. Don't you
realize those things will kill you?

DR. EVIL
Most of life's pleasures are quite toxic. I believe in rotat-
ing your vices. When I go to France, I don't eat red meat, but I
have all the cheese I want. The cheese in France is exquisite.
It's like heroin. I have a rule, however: never eat more in one
sitting than your head weighs. I learned that from the Maoris—

SCOTT
Shut up! Don't you see? He's doing it right now. Doesn't anybody else think he's nuts? Ask him about the nursery rhymes! Go
ahead, ask him!

THERAPIST
Scott tells me that you wrote some nursery rhymes for him.
That's a very good start. May we hear them?

DR. EVIL
Really? All right. Here's one:
    "Hickory Dickory Evil
    The swinger ran up the steeple
    The clock struck five
    he's no longer alive,
    Hickory Dickory Evil"
This one I wrote while having a glass of Cristal. It's the
finest champagne in the world:

"Dr. Evil sat on a wall
Dr. Evil had a great fall
And all the doctor's horses
And all the doctor's men
Couldn't put Dr. Evil together again,
So he had them liquidated."

SCOTT
Hello! Koo-koo! Koo-koo! For one thing, I'm too old for stupid nursery rhymes. For another thing, you're whacked!

THERAPIST
Dr. Evil, it's terrific that you made that effort. Scott is facing a different set of challenges, however. For instance, he's having some trouble at school—

DR. EVIL
School? Oh, I remember school! What a time it was. I was educated by the Benedictines in a remote corner of the Alps. There really is nothing like a German education, you know....

At this point, the recording device failed and the transcription ends. A man gave his life for this tape, and I think we've seen enough to realize that Dr. Evil is a freaked-out square and that world annihilation is his bag. Unfortunately, the only way to fight him is to know how he thinks. Frightening, baby, very frightening indeed!

A Memo from Dr. Evil

TO: Technical staff
FROM: Dr. Evil
RE: Mr. Bigglesworth
cc: Number Two, Frau Farbissina

As you can see in the photographs here, the freezing
and feline reanimation process was quite difficult on
Mr. Bigglesworth. I myself have been turned into a
crippled freak because of the bungling of that incompetent
ingrate Mustafa, former head of the technical staff.
You all know what happened to him.

We have tried a full-body toupee on Mr. Bigglesworth, but
he complained of chafing. Likewise, we found him to
be allergic to Rogaine. You have sensitive skin, don't
you, kitty-witty? Little bitty kitty-witty...Anyway,
I want hair back on my cat! You have fourteen days to find
a solution to this problem. Need I remind you of the cost
of failure?

53

Ministry of
Defense
Personnel Files

Name: Two, Number (no middle)

AKA: "Two," "Deucie," "Patch" (never to his face)
Birthplace: Woodstock, NY
Current Address: Penthouse, Virtucon Towers,
                          Las Vegas
Family Background: parents were very early participants in
                          the utopian communal living experiments
                          which eventually led to the more widely
                          known "hippies"
Prior Arrests: public urination (in college)
Distinguishing Marks: well-tailored suits; one eyeball missing
Modus Operandi: motivated by greed;
                          in Dr. Evil's absence he transformed
                          Virtucon from a simple front company into a
                          multibillion-dollar conglomerate by
                          embracing true evil, i.e., cable television

MOD
FILE 80869

Name: Fagina, Alotta

AKA: Due to years of embarrassment, Alotta had
                            her name changed. She is now known legally
                            as Sandy, Sandy Fagina

Birthplace: Sicily
Current Address: Room 69, El Rancho Mirage Inn,
                            Las Vegas
Family Background: born to peasant farmers in
                            Sicily, her name actually translates
                            to "virgin hope"

Prior Arrests: none
Distinguishing Marks: well, let's see . . .
                            extremely large breasts
                            a shrewd operative who uses her Mediterranean
Modus Operandi: sexuality to get ahead in a man's world

MOD
FILE 30253

56

Name: Farbissina, Frau

AKA:	"Bissy"
Birthplace:	somewhere in East Germany
Current Address:	unknown
Family Background:	an orphan, she was raised in an all-girls school; her limited contact with men makes her partial to female company, if you know what we mean
Prior Arrests:	at seventeen she was remanded to a juvenile prison for girls for breaking the hands of a schoolboy who tried to touch her "cushy pillows"
Distinguishing Marks:	tattoo of Martina Navratilova from that crazy night in Düsseldorf
Modus Operandi:	fiercely loyal to Dr. Evil, who rescued her from a finishing school for criminal girls, Frau really has no interest in makeup, clothes, or men. I don't see how we could be more clear.

MOD
FILE 120449

Name: Boutros-Ghali, Mustafa

AKA: "Moooooooooose!"
Birthplace: Fez, Morocco
Current Address: Queens, NY
Family Background: raised by a traditional Muslim family, Mustafa showed early aptitude for engineering and was a keen reader of <u>Popular Mechanics</u>

Prior Arrests: sentenced to fifty lashes in Yemen for peering at a woman under her veil during the holy month of Ramadan

Distinguishing Marks: sweats profusely
Modus Operandi: lured into Western culture by Dr. Evil's promise of technology unavailable in his homeland, Mustafa is torn between his strict moral code and his love of DIRECTV

Name: O'Brien, Patrick Wallace
        Fitzgerald Seamus

AKA: Patty O'Brien
Birthplace: sod hut in County Clare
Current Address: above Emerald Isle Pub, Dublin
Family Background: father drank like a fish, mother yelled, had
                         about a hundred brothers and sisters
Prior Arrests: drunk and disorderly (multiple); brawling
                         (Cup match versus England)
Distinguishing Marks: a pint of Guinness in his hand
Modus Operandi: a sometimes uneven, but deadly killer,
                         O'Brien always carries a charm which he con-
                         siders lucky (green clover, yellow moons,
                         blue diamonds, etc.)

MOD
FILE 80774

Name:　Kim, Sheung

AKA:　　　　　　　　　　　　　"Random Task"
Birthplace:　　　　　　　　　Seoul, Korea
Current Address:　　　　　　Los Angeles
Family Background:　　　　　raised by Gypsies in the central mountain
　　　　　　　　　　　　　　　region of Romania, Random Task is
　　　　　　　　　　　　　　　well-versed in the songs and folklore
　　　　　　　　　　　　　　　of these fascinating peoples

Prior Arrests:　　　　　　　none
Distinguishing Marks:　　　bears an uncanny resemblance to a
　　　　　　　　　　　　　　　Kenmore refrigerator

Modus Operandi:　　　　　　a hit man for hire, kills with his deadly
　　　　　　　　　　　　　　　flying shoe for the highest bidder

MOD
FILE _20935_

60

Have you hugged an elderly person today?

Virtucon. Good products. Good people.

Virtucon cares about your community. Do you? Have you taken the time lately to hug an elderly person, even if their odor makes you uncomfortable? Have you helped a young child learn to read? Even small gestures can help, like carrying groceries for a busy mother or cleaning graffiti from a public phone. In fact, 1 carrying groceries + 2 cleaning graffitis = 1 hugging an elderly person. Or, looking at it another way, 3 carrying groceries + 4 cleaning graffitis = 1 teaching a child to read. Of course, 1 hugging an elderly person + 3 carrying groceries = 1 teaching a child to read with 1 cleaning graffiti left over. See how easy it really is?

62

The Fembots are Dr. Evil's most diabolical weapon.
Alluring women on the surface, they are killing machines underneath.
I narrowly survived my only face-to-face intercourse with them.
(Behave!)

While searching through the ruins of Dr. Evil's volcano lair,
we found the original schematic diagrams for the Fembots,
with notes in the bad Doctor's handwriting. You might be tempted
to assemble one of these birds yourself. Shag at your own risk.

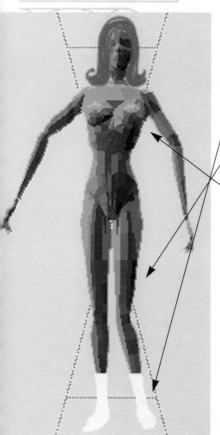

"Good work. These automated strumpets will appeal to any man.
I've made a few notes on items that the
degenerate swinger Austin Powers will not
be able to resist. I expect to see
a prototype in one month.

"The Fembots should all wear white go-go boots. Powers is partial to them.

"Replace legs with longer 'Ursula Andress' variation (part #71-004D).

"Breasts should be larger still. Powers is simpleminded
and can't resist large jobblies.

****** "Very Important:
replace green eyes with blue (part #34-200B)
to match those of Powers's associate, Mrs. Kensington.
Psyche research indicates our little spy is
quite attached to her. This is our secret weapon, gentlemen;
I expect it to perform perfectly!"
                                    —Dr. E

HOW TO MAKE A FEMBOT

3/4"   5/8"   9/16"   1/2"

1/4"   3/16"   3/8"   7/16"

And now, a word from Scott Evil

I was in group therapy with my dad (which is totally bogus because no one there believes he is, like, evil) and the therapist made us promise to do, like, father-and-son junk together. My dad's been out of it for thirty years, so I figured I'd take him to the video store:

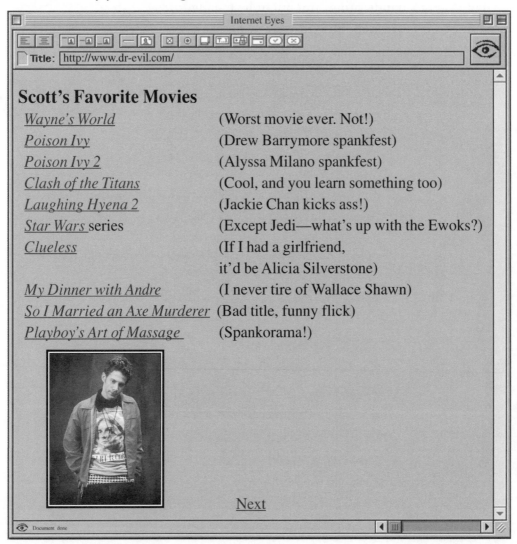

Internet Eyes

Title: http://www.dr-evil.com/

Scott's Favorite Movies

Wayne's World	(Worst movie ever. Not!)
Poison Ivy	(Drew Barrymore spankfest)
Poison Ivy 2	(Alyssa Milano spankfest)
Clash of the Titans	(Cool, and you learn something too)
Laughing Hyena 2	(Jackie Chan kicks ass!)
Star Wars series	(Except Jedi—what's up with the Ewoks?)
Clueless	(If I had a girlfriend, it'd be Alicia Silverstone)
My Dinner with Andre	(I never tire of Wallace Shawn)
So I Married an Axe Murderer	(Bad title, funny flick)
Playboy's Art of Massage	(Spankorama!)

Next

Document done

Title: http://www.dr-evil.com/~10html/drmovies

Dr. Evil's Favorite Movies

<table>
<tr><td>Death Takes a Holiday</td><td>Darkman</td></tr>
<tr><td>Army of Darkness</td><td>Death in Venice</td></tr>
<tr><td>Evil Dead 2</td><td>Death Wish</td></tr>
<tr><td>Babe</td><td>Faces of Death</td></tr>
<tr><td>Death in the Afternoon</td><td>The Sterile Cuckoo</td></tr>
</table>

"Click Here to See My Favorite *Beavis and Butt-Head*"

"Click Here to Join My On-line D&D Game (No Paladins Allowed!)"

"Click Here to Hear the Time I Called in to Howard Stern"

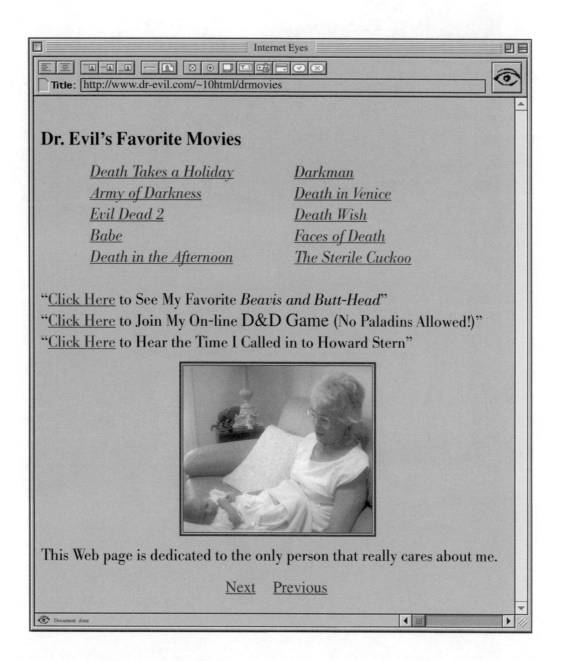

This Web page is dedicated to the only person that really cares about me.

Next   Previous

65

Though I try not to
lord it over other blokes,
I am, in fact, a learned man.
Whilst at university,
I committed much verse
to memory.
Here are a few of
my favorites:

"Pardon me for being rude,
It was not me, it was my food.
It just popped up to say hello,
and now it's gone back down below."

Continuing with the theme
of digestion and other bodily functions
is this classic:

"Milk, milk, lemonade.
Round the corner fudge is made.
Stick your finger in the hole,
And out comes a Tootsie Roll!"

I think it was Wordsworth who penned this little gem:

"Press the button,
Pull the chain,
Out comes a chocolate choo-choo train."

67

PHOTO SHOOT

Although being an International Man of Mystery is my hobby, fashion photography is my daytime gig. It might seem just a gas to jet-set all over the world and take snaps of beautiful birds in erotic poses, but it has its drawbacks. I'll get back to you when I think of one, baby!

JudoChop

I learned my unique style of marital arts while on a spiritual trek through Nepal with George and Ringo in early 1967. One morning the boys were playing sitar around the campfire and, as I had a bit of the headache, I decided to go for a walk. Soon I became lost in the forest. After walking for miles I was nearly dead from exhaustion and dehydration. An older Oriental man found me in this pitiful state and rescued me.

By doing chores for him, such as painting a fence or washing a car, I learned the mystical "Wax On, Wax Off" method of martial arts. At the end of my time there, I asked him, "Master, are you the legendary wise man of Nepal?" He smiled in his all-knowing way and responded, "No, my son, I am Pat Morita of television's *Happy Days*. I'm here on vacation with my wife."

Here's one of the more devastating moves Pat taught me. Handle with care, baby!

70

The Drunken Monkey

A favorite ruse of assassins is to dress like women. Trust me on this, man. I can't tell you how many times in the course of my work as an International Man of Mystery that some cat dressed like a bird has tried to kill me. Literally dozens, baby!

You think it would be easy to tell if a chick is really a man in drag; after all, there are some obvious differences! For example, men have penises, whereas women have two lactating breasts and a vagina. (Although there's a funny thing I've noticed— men also have breasts, but milk doesn't come out of them!)

Anyway, it's easier than you think to be fooled. Here's a quick primer on how to spot a man in drag. It could save your life, baby.

How to Spot a Man in Drag

At first glance, this beauty
might seem quite attractive.
But watch out chaps, she's a he,
and he's deadly, indeed!

Always look at the
hands first.
They're a
dead giveaway,
baby!
Look at 'em—
they're carpenter's
hands!
All the manicures
in the world
can't hide
the fact that
those are
the hands
of a man.

She is
all woman,
baby!
This is a bird
you can take
home to your
mother!
Look at the
hands—
graceful as
you please.
A little large,
granted,
but not
mannish
in the least.

Consider these
breasts.
No real woman has breasts like these.
Gor blimey, they're huge! They're like a shelf!
You could rest a clock on that rack.
No, my friend, someone's been stuffing.

Penis Enlarger Pump

Birds of the World

An International Man of Mystery needs hobbies. Saving the world from evil can be quite stressful, and too much stress will crimp a swinger's style. Anybody who knows me will tell you that one of my favorite hobbies is bird-watching. Of course, the kind of birds I'm talking about don't fly, baby, except maybe in a jumbo jet! Here's a field guide to the world's most shagadelic birds:

Swedish Bird

Distribution:	Lapland, Super 8 films, jumbo jets
Feeding:	pickled herring, vodka
Nesting:	ski lodges, castles
Behavior:	shagging, skiing, and shagging
Plumage:	fur-fringed ski outfits, bikinis

75

French Bird

Distribution:	Paris, Greenwich Village
Feeding:	baguettes, red wine, chocolate, cigarettes
Nesting:	pied-à-terres, châteaux
Behavior:	reading, arguing, smoking
Plumage:	men's overcoats, miniskirts, berets

Oriental Bird

Distribution:	Pacific Rim, Harvard
Feeding:	sushi
Nesting:	hotels
Behavior:	has been known to shop for up to thirty-six hours
Plumage:	traditional: kimono; modern: Chanel

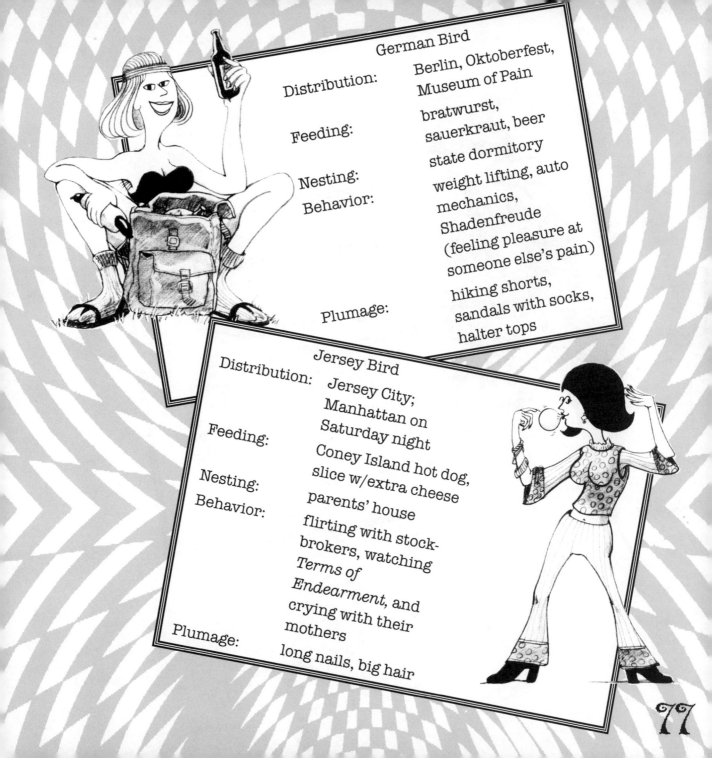

German Bird

Distribution:	Berlin, Oktoberfest, Museum of Pain
Feeding:	bratwurst, sauerkraut, beer
Nesting:	state dormitory
Behavior:	weight lifting, auto mechanics, Shadenfreude (feeling pleasure at someone else's pain)
Plumage:	hiking shorts, sandals with socks, halter tops

Jersey Bird

Distribution:	Jersey City; Manhattan on Saturday night
Feeding:	Coney Island hot dog, slice w/extra cheese
Nesting:	parents' house
Behavior:	flirting with stock-brokers, watching *Terms of Endearment*, and crying with their mothers
Plumage:	long nails, big hair

Pet Bird

Distribution: Australia to
Marks & Spencers'
basement

Feeding: seed, cuttlefish bone

Nesting: cages all over—
South Kensington,
mostly

Behavior: staring into mirror,
thinking it's seeing
another bird

Plumage: green, blue,
and yellow

78

79

HOW TO PICK UP CHICKS

To be an effective International Man of Mystery, you must have a way with the ladies. Sometimes in the line of duty you will be forced to shag some crumpet. Tough job, eh, lads?

The key to picking up chicks, of course, is to be yourself, especially if you're handsome, rich, and powerful. But, what if you're a bit square, or just a little shy? Well, I've assembled some of my most fab pickup lines to help get you over the hump—behave!

Hey baby, what's your sign? (Just for the record, I was the first to use this one.)

How about a quick shag in the toilet? (Low percentage. Use sparingly.)

"Yes, Austin, I'd love to have a shag." (See "How to Hypnotize")

Would you like to see my jumbo jet? (Chicks love a witty chap.)

A shag a day keeps the doctor away.

In my homeland I'm considered quite handsome.

If I said you had a beautiful body, would you hold it against me?

Would you like to go back to my flat and listen to Burt Bacharach records? (Save this one for last. It works every time.)

Shall we shag now, or shall we shag later?

"**THE ULTIMATE SQUARE**"

82

How to Freak Out Squares

Sometimes I'm sitting alone in my loft/photography studio and I get very bored. There's nothing on the BBC, I don't feel like taking any snaps, the Jag's in the shop getting a lube job, whatever. I've just got the blues, you know what I mean?

Just then, who should ring me up but my friend Rod? Now, Rod is so mod that we call him Rod the Mod. He's so mod he makes me look positively square, baby, and that ain't easy to do! He's got the best hi-fi system in London and he rides a groovy Vespa scooter. Rod's the kind of cheeky chappy who always rings you up when you're bored.

"Let's go freak out some squares, man!" he says. "Smashing!" says I, and off we go.

Freaking out squares is one of the best parts of being a swinger. They can't handle the freedom, man—it freaks them out! The grooviest place to go is Trafalgar Square at lunchtime. You get a nice cross-section of squares there. When you're first starting out, you'll want to use phrases like, "Make love, not war!" and "Have you been experienced, baby?" or "Free love now, free love forever!" Later on you can improvise.

There's nothing more uncool than a cat who orders the wrong drink. As a swinger it's your obligation to have a signature bevy, preferably something very groovy. That shaken-not-stirred business is strictly for the squares. For those of us in the know, the drink of choice is the:

Skinny Pirate

Skinny Pirate

$2/3$ Tab diet soda
$1/3$ Myers Rum
In a highball glass mix the Tab and rum over crushed ice.
Note: before pouring, coat inside of glass with the juice from $1/4$ lemon. That's what gives it its zing, baby! Enjoy!

Now, there are some acceptable alternates, in case Tab isn't available (for some inexplicable reason, not all establishments carry it). The first is called a Shandy and it's quite popular in my hometown:

Shandy

Mix the beer of your choice (it could be a stout, an ale, a lager, a pilsner, what have you) with a liberal dose of lime juice.
It might seem strange to you Yanks, but a million Englishmen can't be wrong.

This last drink I would recommend only for the strong of spirit. It's something my grandfather cooked up after his third wife died:

Tommy Dazzler

$1/2$ vodka
$1/2$ gin
No wonder they call it a dazzler, eh? Old Grandpa, he'd have a couple of Tommy Dazzlers with dinner, then he'd start talking to the dog, Ricky. "Ricky," he'd say, "You're a good dog." After two more Tommy Dazzlers, Ricky would tell Grandpa about the great conflagration that was coming to burn up all the sinners and Grandpa would run naked into the bloody streets, shouting. On second thought, do not, I repeat DO NOT, order a Tommy Dazzler.

Remember, a real cool cat never drinks more than he can handle. After all, an International Man of Mystery has to have his wits about him at all times to fight danger, and, if an opportunity presents itself, you'll want to be able to "rise" to the occasion.

Behave!

How to Play the Sitar

One thing that puzzled me about the nineties was that no one was playing the sitar anymore. I looked around and thought, "Isn't anyone interested in exotic stringed instruments played on atonal scales?"

The sitar comes to us from India, a land of great mysticism, spirituality, and curry. I was introduced to the sitar by my friend George Harrison of the Beatles. Now, I'm no Ravi Shankar, but I know a few tunes on the sitar, and I'd be happy to teach you one.

Let's try "Dueling Banjos" (or is it "Dueling Sitars"?) from the classic Burt Reynolds film *Deliverance*. (Am I the only one that thinks this flick is ripe for a remake, baby? Imagine Brad Pitt in Burt's part, Tom Selleck as the other bloke on the raft, and, well, Ned Beatty in Ned Beatty's part. I get a chill just thinking about it, man.)

An International Man of Mystery must be at the top of his form both mentally and physically to fulfill his duties. I myself practice judo and do the *Times* crossword puzzle every Sunday. There is, however, another facet to the complete International Man of Mystery— the spiritual being. To really swing on many planes of existence, you must be a scholar of the mystic arts or mind/body spirituality. I met my guru, the guru Harold, on my travels to Bangladesh with Cat Stevens (whatever happened to him anyway?).

My Guru

HOW TO DRESS LIKE A SWINGER

If you want to be a swinger, you have to look the part. If you're a bit on the square side, don't have a thrombo. I'm quite the fashion plate, and I'll show you how to look like a swinger.

The first rule is, there are no rules, baby! That's what being a swinger's all about—expressing yourself. If it feels good to you, do it. If it looks good to you, wear it, man!

I think this combo is gear,
but only after Labor Day.
You have to draw the line
somewhere, man!

This fab outfit is
perfect for everyday wear,
or you can accessorize for
those dressy occasions!

You can never have
too much color, baby!

Fashion is groovy, man, but
don't change a thing on my PJs!

WE'RE HIRING!

Virtucon is growing, and that means opportunity! If you're looking for something more challenging than the normal 9 to 5 routine, then Virtucon is the place for you!

We especially need computer-aided design artists and henchman. If you're just out of art school, or have even a small amount of experience as a henchman, don't be afraid to call. We offer a paid ten-week henchman's training course and offer a full array of henchman's benefits, including a generous 401(k) plan. If you're not afraid to be killed en masse by the film's hero or run around aimlessly while the evil lair self-destructs, then you'd make the perfect henchman!

Come join our happy and hygienic workplace!

A true International Man of Mystery has many interests. One of my favorite sidelines is my groovy band, Ming Tea. We're a five-man outfit (four men and one bird, actually) not unlike the Rolling Stones, and we've had some wild shindigs all around London. We've even appeared on *Top of the Pops*!

I dig gigging with the band, man, but I try to keep mellow. Remember, as soon as the business starts getting into your headspace, the music dies. Turn the page for the lyrics to our biggest smash yet, out on the Blue Boy recording label.

Here's Ming Tea!
That's me, Austin, on lead
vocals—
hello, hello!
The dashing cat on bass
is Sid Belvedere.
My mate from Manchester,
Trevor Aigberth, handles
lead guitar, while
Gillian Shagwell plays rhythm,
and oh what a rhythm she's got!
Holding everything together is
Manny Stixman on the drums.

Come check us out, baby!

Sexual Revolution

by Ming Tea

There's a sexual revolution,
   you can feel it in the air.

[There's a groovy psychedelic guitar riff in between the lines, man.]

People shagging just like weasels
   and they just don't seem to care.

Hey, watch out, squares—
   you make us bored.

The penis is mightier than the sword!

[Here's where Gillian does this groovy move with her hips. Fab, baby!]

There's a sexual revolution and
   you ain't seen nothing yet—

People shagging in the clubs,
   and inside a jumbo jet.

Hey square world—the end is nigh.

When we say "hump," you say
   "How high?"

Go make love, or masturbate—

Sexual freedom will never be

Out of daaaaaaate!

[I hold this note a smashing long time, opera singer–like, and just when you think it's over, we got into this call-and-response chanting bit here:]

Free—Love!

Free—Love!

Free—Love!

[Here's the last bit. We whip ourselves into a psychedelic frenzy and collapse in a musical orgy. It's wild, man, really wild!]

It's the sixties!

FAB!

Lights!
Camera!
Austin Powers!

97

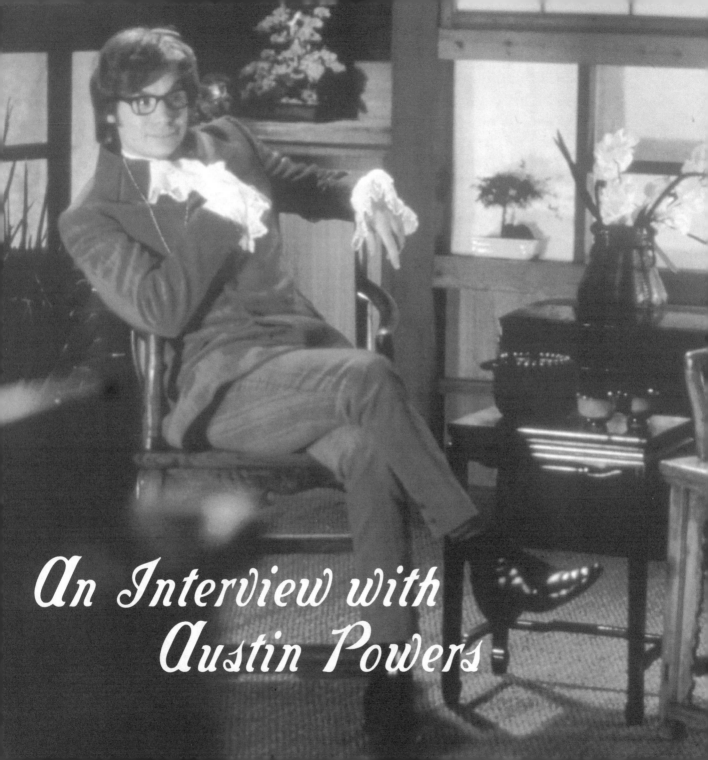

An Interview with
Austin Powers

To help us celebrate our thirtieth anniversary, we're conducting interviews with some of the seminal groovers and shakers that helped make *Fab* magazine *the* chronicle of London's swinging psychedelic scene. Who would have thought in 1967 that our little radical rag would grow into an influential journalistic voice for social change, and then into a self-satisfied arbiter of hipness, and then into a bloated parody of itself, and finally into a giant corporate cog, merging with a multinational media concern, contributing to global cultural hegemony, becoming that which we vowed to mock, and broadcasting nonsense on cable twenty-four hours a day? Quite remarkable. Who better to help us celebrate our "shaggy" roots than the original swinger, Austin Powers?

Interview by Ellen Swellbottom.

E.S.: *What is the first thing you wanted to do after you were unfrozen?*

A.P.: Shag, baby, shag! A nice long shag in a warm tub, perhaps, or a little shaglet in the alley, or a shagorama with multiple birds—

E.S.: *Yes, yes, yes—But what else?*
A.P.: What else? Besides shag? Let me think. . . . Oh yes, I wanted to take a vacation in an exotic tropical paradise, so I gave my travel agent a tinkle on the telling bone to book me a jaunt to Vietnam—the French grub is outstanding there, baby! There was some crazy snafu, something about land mines, so I says how about a nice ski trip, someplace mountainous and cold with a nice covering of the white stuff? The Balkans, say? Well, that was no go either. But some bloke named Eisenhower or Eisner or something gave me a paper bag full of dosh—so I'm going to Disneyland!

E.S.: *What did it feel like to be frozen?*
A.P.: Well, love, it's hard to talk about it. It was . . . brutal . . . very . . . [*breaks down*]. I don't think I can go on. [*Composes himself*]. It was very, very . . . cold. Not unlike skinny dipping in the Thames in December, only worse. My bits and pieces had retreated well up

into my abdominal cavity, baby! And that ain't groovy!

E.S.: *Since the Cold War is over, many people would say there's no place in the nineties for an International Man of Mystery. How would you respond?*
A.P.: I would say to such a person—"you've got a little blob of something on your tie" and I would point to their tie, just at the sternum. "Hello, hello" they might say, then, when they looked down, I'd bring my finger up with great force and thump their bloody nose with it! No place indeed!

E.S.: *How do you feel about the way the very notion of celebrity has changed since the sixties?*
A.P.: I'm not political, baby. I don't understand the question. I didn't realize we were in an intellectual salon.

E.S.: *You lived through a very tumultuous time, with changing sexual mores and social upheaval. What advice can you offer young people today who face similar questions?*
A.P.: Always shower before *and* after a shag.

E.S.: *It seems all you ever think about is sex. Don't you realize that your very modes of expressing erotic desire are dated?*
A.P.: I don't know what you're talking about, baby, but it's making me very horny!

E.S.: *I can assure you that is not my intent.*

Let's go on with the interview.
A.P.: Oh, I'm definitely horny now, baby. Randy, indeed! You've got quite a nice figure, Ms. Swellbottom.

E.S.: *What's your opinion on the declining political stability in the former U.S.S.R., and do you think it desirable to allow former Iron Curtain nations to join NATO?*
A.P.: Would you like to shag?

E.S.: *What?*
A.P.: Would you? Would you fancy a shag? I'd fancy one rotten!

E.S.: *No, no thank you. Just answer the question.*
A.P.: I drive a Shaguar, you know. Very erotic.

E.S.: *All right, moving on. One of the greatest foreign policy challenges facing the West is the rise of militant Islamic Nationalism in the Middle East. Is there anything we can do to protect our strategic interests on the Arabian Peninsula?*
A.P.: Did you say peninsula? Doesn't that word make you horny? It makes me randy, indeed, just the sound of it. To me, it's Eros made manifest. Doesn't it make you the least bit horny? I'm getting ants in me pants. Don't you have any blood in your veins? Hey, where are you going? Don't walk away, the party's just getting started. Aren't you horny? Does this mean you don't want to shag?